CW01499975

Feng Shui Your Wallet and Purse for Prosperity

Feng Shui Prosperity Secrets Series Book 1

Diana Loera

Copyright 2015 All rights reserved

Without limiting the rights under the copyright reserved above, no part of this book may be reproduced, stored in or introduced into a retrieval system, or transmitted, in any form, or by any means (electronic, mechanical, photocopying, recording, or otherwise) without the prior written permission of Diana Loera and Loera Publishing LLC.

Book piracy and any other forms of unauthorized distribution or use without written permission by Diana Loera/Loera Publishing LLC will be prosecuted to the fullest extent of the law.

The author neither implies nor promises that you will achieve the desired results listed herein. This book contains information gained from Feng Shui experts, research and personal experience. Each person's results will vary.

Other Books by Diana Loera

12 Extra Special Summer Dessert Fondue Recipes http://tinyurl.com/q7gpgw8

Fast Start Guide to Flea Market Selling http://tinyurl.com/qb83smw

14 Extra Special Winter Holidays Fondue Recipes http://tinyurl.com/lkebggx

Awesome Thanksgiving Leftovers Revive Guide http://tinyurl.com/prxjayg

Stop Hot Flashes Now http://tinyurl.com/kxmr8ps

Party Time Chicken Wing Recipes http://tinyurl.com/ohsc9x8

Summertime Sangria http://tinyurl.com/oxnlnhm

Please visit www.LoeraPublishingLLC.com to see our complete selection of books.

Topics include cooking, travel, recipes, how to, non- fiction and more.

Table of Contents

Introduction

Thank you very much for reading my book. I'm always looking for interesting topics and recipes to share with readers.

The idea for this book came to me earlier this year and as 2015 marches towards a close, I wanted to publish this book which is the first of my books on various Feng Shui topics.

I've have an interest in Feng Shui for years and in 2001 had a Feng Shui consultant go through my home and offer insight regarding energy flows.

In looking back, it was a bit overwhelming to have a detailed list of numerous things in my home that I should change but I did it. I forgot a lot of what I did and maybe more important, why I did it. I think it was just an overload of too much new information at one time.

I think that perhaps offering Feng Shui improvements in smaller steps may be a better for many people, including myself.

My idea was to create smaller Feng Shui steps that one can implement faster and also create books that are faster reads as they cover just one area of Feng Shui improvement.

Starting with something as simple as a wallet gives one some insight on Feng Shui and is something that can be done fairly fast.

Prosperity is a very hot topic now, maybe even more so the past few years due to our rollercoaster economy.

In this book we'll cover what one needs to do to ensure that their wallet, and purse if you use one, are set up in accordance with Feng Shui planning for prosperity.

I have capitalized the words Feng Shui throughout. In some of my research I noticed it wasn't capitalized and in some cases it was, so to keep it uniform in this book I capitalized it.

In some cases, such as if you should place credit cards in your wallet, I went with the majority of feedback from Feng Shui experts.

What is Feng Shui?

I think that most readers have an idea about Feng Shui but in the event that it is a new topic for a reader, I am going to share the basics of what Feng Shui is and also a brief history of Feng Shui before we progress to the main topic of this book.

Feng Shui is a Chinese philosophical system of harmonizing everyone with the surrounding environment. If everything is harmonized there is less stress and more flow.

Feng Shui focuses on invisible forces that bind the universe, earth and humanity together. This fore is known as qi.

In this book you may see the word auspicious used.

Auspicious means something that is favorable, something that is conductive to success. It is a word used commonly by Feng Shui experts and consultants.

Interestingly enough, Feng Shui was suppressed in mainland China in the 1960's. It has once again increased in popularity and is very popular in the US.

Feng Shui consultants are available to come to your home and office to consult with you regarding the placement of objects and how they affect the qi.

In some cases you may be able to move an object that has blocked qi, thus opening the flow channel back up.

In other cases, if it is a structural problem that cannot be physically changed or move, the Feng Shui consultant will offer remedies such as the use of a mirror to help you with the problem.

History of Feng Shui

Feng Shui's history goes back as far as 5,000 years. It was practiced during the Tang Dynasty and there are early recordings about employing Feng Shui masters in selecting auspicious sites, as well as Feng Shui texts being required reading for imperial exams in the court of Emperor Hi Tsang, 888 A.D.

One of the most famous Feng Shui names recorded in the history of Feng Shui is Master Yang Yun Sang, who left a legacy of many classical Feng Shui texts and is considered the founder of the landscape school of Feng Shui.

Almost a hundred years later, another Feng Shui school of thought - the Compass Feng Shui School - gained strength and popularity.

The main influence in this Feng Shui school was the Feng Shui master named Wang Chih who developed his teachings during the Song Dynasty.

The Compass Feng Shui School calculations are based on the compass directions and the I-Ching trigrams arranged in the octagonal symbol of the bagua, or Feng Shui energy map.

In late nineteenth century, after a period of existence as two separate schools, the two Feng Shui schools of thought - the Landscape, or Form Feng Shui School, and the Compass Feng Shui School - merged, thus providing for a body of knowledge of unique depth and wisdom in reading the energy in any space, be it home, office or garden.

Feng Shui has gained in popularity and it is now more common than ever before for people to use the tools of Feng Shui to enhance their home and work environment.

Feng Shui and Prosperity

One wants to be able to allow the energy of wealth into their home or office. This also applies to your wallet and purse.

Having blocked channels doesn't allow the proper energy flow and you even may be unknowingly doing something that blocks prosperity and draws debt towards you, not prosperity.

With wallet and purses many people have a tendency to cram a variety of non- money items into both, thus according to Feng Shui experts, blocking the qui.

In this book we are going to walk through the prosperity steps suggested by Feng Shui experts regarding wallets and purses.

Feng Shui Your Wallet and Purse for Prosperity

In the following pages we will walk through the Feng Shui process for wallets and then purses.

The advice herein was provided by several Feng Shui experts.

Getting Started

With Feng Shui one believes that our attitude towards money determines money's attitude towards us.

If we treat our money well, money flows towards us. If we treat our money poorly, or like trash, it doesn't flow and one is always lacking in financial means or draws debt towards themselves.

Clutter-free energy, order and beauty have to be present for good Feng Shui.

To start we're going to take a look at your wallet and if you use a purse, we're also discussing purses later in this book.

If chosen and treated correctly, the right wallet may be a powerful Feng Shui tool for attracting wealth, money and prosperity in to your life.

Please try to read this book when you have the time to go through the steps without rushing or read through it now and then plan on going back and actually doing the steps when you are not rushed.

Let's start with your wallet.

Take it out of your purse or pocket and examine it. This is not a make wrong exercise, so if your wallet is falling apart and full of gum wrappers and receipts, that's okay. We're going to make some changes.

Think about how you feel when you look at your wallet.

Do you dread looking inside?

Do you spend time fumbling through your wallet when you are at the store since you have so many receipts and non- money items in your wallet?

Are receipts hanging out of your wallet?

Open up your wallet and look inside.

What is the first thing that you see?

What is the main thing that you see?

How does it make you feel when you look inside your wallet?

Take the contents out of your wallet and sort them into piles – receipts, credit cards, cash, membership/loyalty cards, photos, garbage and other miscellaneous stuff.

Feng Shui experts say that money doesn't like to be crowded.

If you're like most people, your money has been packed in to your wallet in with a wide assortment of other stuff.

Kind of like a person being on a train in the middle of rush hour – packed like a sardine.

Packed like a sardine on a sultry August afternoon – you may know that feeling and it isn't pleasant.

Your money is experiencing that same discomfort as it is jostled among gun wrappers and old receipts.

Now we are going to follow the Feng Shui path and make a few changes.

Ideally, the only thing going back in your wallet is the cash. Realistically speaking, you may need to keep your driver's license in your wallet, if so, place it in a section divided away from your money.

If your wallet has a divider, you can, for the time being until you get a new wallet, put the credit cards you absolutely must have with you, on the other side of the divider.

Credit cards represent debt and money owed, so you can see why we don't want them in with your money. Ideally, when you find your new wallet, which we will be discussing soon, your credit cards will not be in the same wallet as your money.

Photos are going elsewhere, just not in your wallet with your cash money. Make sure not to keep family pictures in your wallet. Personal pictures will 'confuse' and 'distract' the money and keep it away from your wallet.

If you feel you must carry photos, consider getting a keychain that holds a photo or one of the digital ones that holds multiple photos.

Receipts signify money spent and debt. They should not be in your wallet – ever.

Feng Shui experts say that having receipts in your wallet is creating the flow to attract more debt which is not what we want to do.

:

Recap of What Should Be In Your Wallet

To recap what we just read, we want our money to feel uncrowded and not be in a cluttered area.

You should always have money in your wallet. Ideally you should have at least one hundred dollar bill in your wallet that you do not spend.

If you've been relying solely on debit cards, you need to go back to using cash and paying with cash.

There should be room for more money as the belief is if there is room for more money that is the message that is being sent out to the Universe.

We want to make sure the following are Not in a wallet -

There should not be receipts in your wallet.

Never use your wallet as a holding area for scraps of paper, candy or gum wrappers or any other junk.

There should not be photos in your wallet

Ideally there should not be credit cards in your wallet. Worse case is that they are divided off in your wallet away from your money. Best case is that they are not in your wallet.

The Best Colors for a Wallet and Why

When we discuss the best colors soon you'll also see one of five elements listed after the color.

When applying Feng Shui, we are also working with the five elements –

Wood, Earth, Metal, Fire and Water.

Wood Element. The wood element represents growth and creativity. Wood fosters personal growth and increases intuition.

Earth Element. The earth element helps to ground and stabilize. Of all the Feng Shui elements, earth is the most peaceful, calming, and stable.

Metal Element. The metal element is related to mental power and sharpness. Metal influences intelligence.

Fire Element. The fire element represents transformation and expansion. Fire is the most volatile of all the five Feng Shui elements.

Water Element. The water element is very useful for release and renewal. Use this element for clarity, inspiration, relaxation, and for letting things go.

While there are wallets available in every shade. I've focused on the most popular shades and why they are or are not the right color choice.

Black Water   Black represents wealth and prosperity. It also is ideal if you are looking for advancement in your career or improving your business

Blue   Water Blue symbolizes money will be drained just like water and also is an attractor for unnecessary splurging making it difficult to accumulate wealth. As you probably already determined, blue is not recommended for your wallet.

Red   Fire   Red represents fire and is not advisable for wallet color because it will burn away your wealth potential. However, red is recommended as a good color for a purse as it activates the flow of money into it and then into your wallet. We will discuss this more later when we discuss purses.

Brown Earth   If you want to increase savings or have a habit of spending too much money, this color may help you to save money.

Pink   Fire   Pink is more suitable for those who are looking for romance as it increases love and relationship luck. If you want to increasing wealth, do not use this color for your wallet.

Green   Wood   Green represents growth and life. A green wallet will help to increase income opportunity. It is especially suitable for entrepreneurs to welcome new business opportunities and ideas.

Yellow   Metal A light yellow color wallet may attract money, but the money will frequently flow both in and out. Mustard yellow will help you to save money. Pastel yellow will help with increasing your wealth luck, attracting stability, reliability and confidence.

Gold   Metal   Gold is associated with luxury and wealth and will help to attract them into your life.

Ideally, Feng Shui experts recommend using a black wallet.

The Condition of Your Wallet

Let's say you already happen to have a black wallet. You've just cleaned it out and organized your cash. So is this exercise done?

Not quite.

Your wallet's condition is a reflection of how you feel regarding money.

Is your wallet ten years old or even older?

Is it beat up and/or discolored?

Does looking at your wallet bring back bad memories or feelings?

Start anew and buy a new wallet.

Since you are starting fresh, look for a wallet that doesn't fold your money.

With a men's wallet, yes you will end up folding the wallet in half but that is not the same as some of the small men's wallets that crimp the bills.

Find a new wallet that resonates well with you and make sure it has plenty of space for cash bills.

Other Feng Shui Money and Prosperity Tips

Feng Shui experts say money doesn't like to be crowded and cramped.

Organize your cash by denomination in your wallet.

Carry a hundred dollar bill in your wallet to attract more hundred dollar bills.

Place your credit cards elsewhere and not in with your cash.
Credit cards symbolize debt not wealth as they signify that you owe debt.

Be careful where you place your wallet. If you just toss it anywhere when you come home, it signifies that you do not care too much about it or the contents – your money.

You must treat your wallet well before they treat you well too. Allocate a special location in your house for your wallet and place it there everything you are back home, so that they will feel treasured. Once you learn to appreciate them, it will tend to attract more money onto your life. Avoid tossing your wallet away on the dining table or anywhere that you find it convenient.

Find a clean, specific place to keep your wallet.

Use cash versus a debit card as much as possible. Recognize the significance of your purchases. Every time that you purchase something from a store, you are validating that business. Handing over money to companies that disrespect their customers or employees, is also showing disrespect to your money.

Applying Fung Shui to Your Purse

As with your wallet, there are recommended steps to take to attract wealth via your purse.

As we did with your wallet we are going to take a hard look at your purse. No tidying up beforehand.

If you're like me, this might be a very eye opening step. Over the years, I've tried keeping my purse somewhat organized but usually within a week, the inside of my purse looked like a herd of wild elephants had ran in and out of it and maybe a group of crazed Jumanji movie monkeys too.

Does the photo below look somewhat familiar? Loose change scattered, cash haphazardly in and out of your wallet, maybe some crumbled tissues, a handful of old receipts, maybe a gum wrapper or two?

The problem, according to Feng Shui experts is our messy purse may be driving wealth luck away from us. Cluttered purses signify confusion. Piles of receipts signify debt and blowing money.

If you had a choice of where to spend a wonderful vacation and were shown two hotels – one was clean, organized and beautiful and the other looked like a cyclone had barreled through, with garbage strewn all over – which one would you choose?

Money is an energy and it reacts to positive and negative energy flows. Clean and spacious areas attract a good money flow. Junky and cluttered block the flow.

Let's start with step one in your purse re-organization and then we'll progress through the rest of the steps –

Ensure that you have uninterrupted time and an area to work, ideally a table or your bed. I highly suggest spreading a towel or plastic garbage bag over the area you will be using.

I also suggest having a wastebasket and possibly some zip lock bags nearby.

Carefully dump the contents onto your work area, removing any highly fragile items first. If you remove any highly fragile items, set them in the work area alongside the contents from your purse.

Starting with the easiest part, throw away trash that is in your purse.

Turn your purse inside out and brush into the wastebasket any crumbs and other bits of debris.

Sort the following into separate piles – this is where the zip lock bags come in handy-

Coins, receipts, make up and anything else that is loose in your purse needs to be separated.

Coins will be going back in your purse but they will be in a coin purse. We will be discussing coin purses soon. First, we are going to discuss purses a bit more.

Purse Choices and Colors

Purses come in every color imaginable. You may change your purses often to match shoes and outfits or you may stay with the same purse no matter what you are wearing.

Color wise, you can utilize the same chart that we used earlier for wallets but what about other purses in various prints and shades?

Remember that money likes to feel valued and safe in a special place. You have already chosen your wallet, now you need a purse to place your wallet in.

While I tend to stay with the traditional black purse most times, I also have my red "power statement" purse and two purses that are considerably flashier than others.

One purse has a black and white zebra pattern and in the middle is a deep rose pink flower with large rhinestones. It is a beautiful and flashy purse. I feel good carrying it and I think my money feels good being carried around in it.

Another purse is a deep summery coral that also has flashy jewels on the outside. I feel good when I carry it and I think my money also feels good being in this purse.

Red is a very auspicious color considered to attract wealth and abundance. The color of the Fire feng shui element with its illumination energy, red is often the favorite feng shui wallet color choice of many die-hard feng shui fans.

However, red being a super-activating color, be mindful that it can energize both positive, as well as your negative traits toward money (somewhat similar to burning the negative traits in a short and intense amount of time), so trust your better judgement and see if you are ready for a red wallet.

With this being said, a black wallet in a red purse may bring a better Feng Shui balance for you.

As with your wallet, you want your purse to be in excellent condition and well maintained.

I have a black purse that I love. I've received countless compliments on it but now where the purse straps connect with metal rings, the straps are wearing.

I could probably continue to use my purse for a while longer but it is not a smart Feng Shui move.

Instead, I've switched purses. I may take my purse to be repaired but if the end result isn't as good as new, I won't continue to use the purse.

How to Take Care of Your Purse in the Feng Shui Manner

Never place your purse on the floor in a washroom.

When dining out, do not place your purse on the floor.

Remember this Feng Shui tip – a purse on the floor = money out the door.

Feng Shui experts state that placing your purse on the floor says to your money that you do not respect it.

Plus, Feng Shui or not, washroom floors are germ havens. After all, would you place your child or yourself on the floor of a washroom? I think not.

You can purchase purse hooks to keep your purse off the floor.

Managing Coins in the Feng Shui Manner

If you are like many people, myself included, you end up with a lot of coins in the bottom of your purse.

Several years ago when I was commuting daily to Chicago, I emptied my purse one weekend as it was feeling unusually heavy. I had over fifty dollars in change scattered in my purse – you read that right – fifty dollars in coins.

With Feng Shui, the belief is that money treats you like you treat it.

So if you are just tossing coins into your purse, you are not respecting the money. You are not giving money a proper, safe and clean area.

Money needs to have its own special place be it a wallet or coin purse, it has a designated place.

Coins need to be placed in a coin purse. I had a coin purse as I used to use one somewhat before. It is purple in color and a decent size.

Purple is considered an auspicious color in Feng Shui and also happens to be my favorite color so having a purple coin purse was a good choice for me.

Purple while auspicious is recommended to use sparingly in Feng Shui so having the color as a coin purse works well as it is smaller than my wallet.

As with your wallet, your coin purse needs to be a decent size as money doesn't like to be crowded and there should be room for more money in your wallet and coin purse.

When your con purse starts to become full, cash the coins in at the bank or move the overflow to a Feng Shui ideal place. I have a crystal barrel shaped jar for my coins at home.

Again, remember, according to Feng Shui, money likes to know it is respected.

Having a designated place for your spare change is a must. Don't just toss it in a drawer.

Occasionally you will come across a wallet with a compartment for coins but I've found the compartment to be quite small so going with a coin purse is a smart Feng Shui move.

When you are at the store, it will become a habit to open your purse, take out your coin purse and place loose change in it when you pay for purses using cash.

The End Result

My end result Feng Shui or not, organization of my purse and wallet has made me feel much better.

My purse is very organized.

When I go in to a store and pay, I am no longer fumbling for my wallet in my purse and then no longer digging through my wallet.

I throw receipts away that I don't need and those that I may need now go in a zip lock bag as soon as I am home.

I never put the receipts in my purse like I used to do.

When I open my purse and wallet, the areas look spacious not cluttered.

I will say, I feel much better about myself after applying the Feng Shui prosperity steps to my purse and wallet.

Coincidence or Feng Shui at Work?

Once you have applied Feng Shui to your purse and/or wallet, I'd love to hear your stories. Please feel free to email me loerapublishing@hotmail.com Please type the words Feng Shui in the subject line.

I receive a lot of emails every day. If a week goes by, with no response from me, kindly re-send it to me as perhaps I missed it or it landed in my spam. Thank you.

Below are some stories to share with you -

I have had several compliments about my purse a few days after I did the Feng Shui process. I found this interesting as although my purse is fairly new, until I did the Feng Shui process no one had commented on my purse. Coincidence or Feng Shui at work?

I went to the grocery store and dollar store and spent about 15.00 at each one. Upon arriving home, my husband walked in behind me and handed me an envelope with thirty dollars cash in it that someone had owed us for a long time. Coincidence or Feng Shui at work?

I do freelance work. Upon finishing the Feng Shui exercise on my wallet and purse, out of the blue, a client emailed and asked if I could handle more work – double the work. Which meant double the money. Coincidence or Feng Shui at work?

My business has been very good this year but we are now approaching the season where my business slows down. Upon doing the Feng Shui process on my wallet, within the week I had a call for an estimate. I gave three quotes as I always do and the client insisted on the largest package which never happens. I didn't even sell as I usually do after the client reads the proposal. The client simply said they wanted the largest package. Coincidence or Feng Shui at work?

I did the Feng Shui process on my wallet. Two days later I had a new client sign up for a large project. They asked for payment terms which were granted. The next day they called and said never mind, they would just pay in full immediately. In my line of work this had never happened before. Coincidence or Feng Shui at work?

I did the Feng Shui process on my wallet and purse. I had been looking for a good used car as the transmission was going out on mine. Within two weeks, I saw a red Cadillac at a car dealership. It was like new and fully loaded. I bought it for way less than I expected and it rides like a dream. Coincidence or Feng Shui at work?

My mom and I both did the Feng Shui process on our purses and wallets. Within a week, my boss told me he would be able to give me a pay increase. I hadn't asked for one. A couple days after that, with no advance notice, he asked me if my mom might be interested in some part time work through the winter months. Coincidence or Feng Shui at work?

My husband did the Feng Shui on his wallet. Later that day a friend who had owed him money for so long that my husband had forgotten about it, called my husband and said he would be bringing the money by in the evening. Coincidence or Feng Shui at work?

These are just a few of the stories about increased cash flow or money owed suddenly returned. Are these just coincidences or are they the effect of Feng Shui at work? Only you can determine what you think about these situations.

I will add this, even if you don't believe in Feng Shui, I think you will appreciate having a very organized purse and wallet.

Closing Comments and Reminders about Feng Shui and Prosperity

Your wallet is the home for your money.

If you have applied Feng Shui in your home, you know there are certain principles that just have to be respected in order to create good Feng Shui.

The same basics will apply for your wallet – clutter-free energy, order and beauty have to be present for good Feng Shui.

I'm sure you've seen people whose wallets are bursting at the seams and overflowing with old receipts, photos and cards that are rarely used. Maybe this was how your own wallet looked.

A cluttered wallet speaks of poverty, scattered energy, fear and chaos, the exact opposite of the energy that is open and ready to receive wealth.

Make sure your wallet stays clean and organized.

Your wallet is a more than just a convenience to hold your money. It is your money's home.

 Money and wealth in general does not like negligent or careless treatment – your wallet should reflect that, so make sure to keep it safe.

Money and wealth are attracted to people who treat it respectfully, with gratitude and appreciation, so keep your wallet in a special place when you get home – don't just throw it down on a random table or dresser.

You should always know where your wallet is and be able to put your hands on it quickly without thinking about it whereabouts - luxury and prosperity are attracted to places, where they "feel" safe.

According to Feng Shui experts treating your wallet this way may make a huge positive impact on your financial position.

Thank you

Thank you very much for taking the time to read my book.

I am not a Feng Shui expert and I appreciate the insight and help from Feng Shui experts who answered my countless questions about Feng Shui and prosperity.

Their patience and wealth of knowledge is what made this book a reality.

I wish you the very best on your path to prosperity.

Sincerely,

Diana

CPSIA information can be obtained at www.ICGtesting.com
Printed in the USA
LVIW01n1421121017
552171LV00011B/86